THE TITLES ARE IN THIS ORDER ON THE CASSETTE:

ISBN 0-7935-2534-9

LAURA WARD, pianist, has been pianist and coach at the Ravinia Festival, and has performed in recital with singers and players nationwide. She has served on the faculty of the Music Academy of the West in Santa Barbara, after studying vocal accompanying there with Gwendolyn Doldofsky. Ms. Ward holds degrees from Baylor University, the Cincinnati Conservatory of Music, and a doctoral degree from the University of Michigan, where she studied with Martin Katz. She also recorded accompaniments for "Italian Tenor Arias."

G. SCHIRMER, Inc.

Distributed by

Hal Leonard Publishing Corporation

7777 West Bluemound Road P.O. Box 13819 Milwaukee, WI 53213

The Beatitudes

Matthew: V, 3-6

ALBERT HAY MALOTTE

ten.
mp
p
en.
Bless -
ten.
p
espr.
mp
ten.
rit.
p
ed   are they   that   mourn:—   for they shall be
pp
rit.
pp
ten.   pp
com -   - fort - ed.
pp   ten.
ral - len - tan - do
p
pp
morendo
Ped.   p Ped.   Ped.   Ped. sostenuto

Lento assai ♩= 50
rit.
rit.
p
a tempo
p
a tempo
p
Bless - ed are the meek: for
they shall in - her - it the earth.
rit.
Ped.
Ped.

p
Bless - ed are
espr. ten. ten.
p p
mp mf rit. f
they which do hun - ger and thirst af - ter right-eous - ness:
mp mf f
rit.
p mp rit. p ral - len - tan - do
for they shall be filled.
ral - len - tan - do l. h.
pp
mp p
lento assai mp p
p ppp
Ped. sostenuto

Create in Me a Clean Heart, O God

Psalm 51: 10-13

CARL MUELLER

spir-it with-in______ me.
cresc.
p sempre
mf
mf
Cast me not a - way from Thy pres -
dim. e rit.
ence; and take not Thy ho - ly spir-it from me.
dim. e rit.

Poco animato
Re - store un - to me the joy of Thy sal - va -tion, re -
store the joy, re - store un - to me the
joy of Thy sal - va -tion; and up - hold me, up - hold

poco cresc.
ff
allarg.
me with Thy free spir - it, Thy free spir - it.
poco cresc.
ff
allarg.
Moderato
f
mf
Then will I teach trans-gres-sors Thy ways; and sin-ners shall be con-
f
mf
rit. e dim.
p
Più lento
pp molto espressione
ppp
vert - ed un - to Thee. Cre - ate in me a clean heart, O God!
rit. e dim.
p
pp
molto espressione
ppp

Ev'ry Time I Feel the Spirit

Spiritual, arranged by HALL JOHNSON

to Verses
Finish
broaden
pray.
Yes ev - 'ry
pray.
p 1. On de
pray.
p 2. Jer - d'n
mf 3. Ain't but
broaden
Verses
moun - tain   my   Lord   spoke,   Out o' His   mouth came   fire   an'
riv - er   chill - y   an'   col',   Chills   de   bod - y   but not de
one train   on   dis   track,   Runs   to   Heav - en   an' runs right
smoke.   In   de   val - ley,   on   my   knees,   Ask'   my
soul.   All   a - roun'   me   look   so   shine,   Ask'   my
back.   Saint Pe - ter   wait - in'   at   de   gate   Says, "Come on,
Lord   have   mer - cy,   please.
Lord   if   all   was   mine.
sin - ner,   don't   be   late".
Yes   ev - 'ry
D.S. %

I Walked Today Where Jesus Walked

Daniel S. Twohig*

GEOFFREY O'HARA

*Words used by exclusive permission

lit - tle lanes, they have not changed— A sweet peace fills the
air. I walked to-day where Je - sus walked, And
felt His pres - ence there. My

Allegretto
mf
path-way led through Beth - le - - hem, Ah! mem-'ries
ev - - - er sweet; The
lit - tle hills of Gal - i - lee, That knew those
child - - - ish feet; The

Mount of Ol - ives: hal - lowed scenes That Je - sus
knew be - fore; I
saw the might - y Jor - dan roll As in the
days of yore.
marcato
f marcato
f rit. e
rit. e
15

I knelt to-day where Je-sus knelt,______ Where
all a-lone He prayed; The Gar - den of Geth-sem-a-
ne ____________ My heart felt un - a - fraid! I
picked my heav-y bur-den up,____________ And with Him by my

poco a poco accel. e cresc.
poco a poco accel. e cresc.
side,_______ I climbed the Hill of Cal - va - ry, I
climbed the Hill of Cal - va - ry, I climbed the Hill of
rit. f molto rall.
ff molto rall.
p
Cal - va - ry,___ Where on the Cross He died!___________ I
rit.
a tempo tranquillo
pp
p a tempo tranquillo
walked to-day where Je - sus walked And felt Him close to me!
pp

I Wonder As I Wander

JOHN JACOB NILES

*In the version of John Jacob Niles, included in "Songs of the Hill Folk", published by G. Schirmer, Inc.

mp a tempo
a tempo
mp
When Ma - ry birthed Je - sus, 'twas in a cow's stall, With

f
f
wise men and farm-ers and shep-herds and all. But high from God's heav-en a

mp   rit.   f   più lento   p
mp   rit.   f   più lento   p
star's light did fall, And the prom-ise of a - ges it then did re-call.

If Je - sus had want - ed for an - y wee thing, A
star in the sky, or a bird on the wing, Or all of God's an - gels in
heav'n for to sing, He sure - ly could have it, 'cause he was the King.

I won-der as I wan-der, out un-der the sky, How
Je-sus the Sav-ior did come for to die For poor on-'ry peo-ple like
you and like I... I won-der as I wan-der, out un-der the sky.

The Lord's Prayer

ALBERT HAY MALOTTE

a tempo
accel.
Bb
poco più mosso
G min
D7
G7 dim.
p
Name.
Thy king - dom
poco più mosso
a tempo
pp
accel.
p
3
3
2 Ped.
Ped.
Dm
Gm
mp
Cm
C#7 dim
D
D7
p
come.
Thy will be done in
p mp
poco cresc.
p
Ped.
Ped.
Ped.
Gm
Eb
p
Bb Gm Dm
Bb
Cm7
F7
Bb
Tempo Iº
p
earth, As it is. in heav - - en.
pp
p
p
p p
p
p
Ped. Ped. Ped.

L'istesso tempo
Eb Bb Eb Bb Gm
p
pp molto espressivo e sempre legato
Eb F7 Bb Eb Bb Eb 6 Bb Gm
pp
Give us this day our
pp
right hand
Eb/G F7 Bb Gm 6 poco accel. A
p p p p
dai - ly bread. And for-give us our debts, As
tres-pass-es As
p r.h. p p poco accel. p
r.h.
l.h.
Ped.

Gm
Gm 6
ral-len-tan-do
A
a tempo
Gm 6
we_____ for-give our debt - ors.
we for-give those who tres-pass a-gainst us.
ral-len-tan-do
a tempo
pp
p
Ped.
Ped.
A
p
Bbmaj 7
Cm
C 7
mf
And lead us not in-to temp-ta - tion; But de - liv-er us from
p
mp
mp
mf
Ped.
F
F 7
Bb 7
Poco meno mosso, e sonoramente
Dm
Bb
Eb maj 7
Cm 7
mf rit.
f
e - vil: For thine is the king - dom,____ and the
mf rit.
f
Ped.
Ped.
(b)
(b)
Ped.

Gm6   C7   ten.   ff   E♭m6   G♭aug   E♭m6
pow - er, and the glo - ry, for
B♭   Gm7   B♭maj7   B♭   Cm7   f   F9   F7
ev - - - er. A -
and ev - er. A -
Tempo I°   mf   p   E♭ B♭ E♭   B♭   E♭ B♭ Cm7 B♭
men.
men.
ral - len - tan - do e morendo
mf   p   pp   ppp
Ped.

Song of Devotion

Text adapted from Philippians I:3-11

JOHN NESS BECK

And this I pray, that your love may a - bound yet more and more_ in
poco a poco cresc.
knowl-edge and in all judg-ment, that ye may ap-prove things that are ex-cel-lent, that
poco a poco cresc.
ye may be sin - cere,_be-ing filled with the fruits of right-eous-ness_ un-to the
ff
glo-ry and praise of God. ___
pp
ff

I thank my God on ev-'ry re-
mem - brance of you, al-ways in ev-'ry prayer of mine for
you with joy; I have you in my heart,
I have you in my heart.

Prayer of the Norwegian Child

Olaf Trojörgson

RICHARD KOUNTZ

Poco più mosso
mf
poco rit
Lord Je - sus, think on me; Make my soul like un-to Thee.
mf
poco rit.
p a tempo
Lord Je - sus, think on me; Make my soul
p a tempo
1. rit.
like un-to Thee.
2. rit.
like un-to Thee.
rit.
rit.

Prayer Perfect

JAMES WHITCOMB RILEY

OLEY SPEAKS

Scat - ter ev - 'ry care ____ Down a wake of an - gel wings
Win - now - ing the air. Dear Lord, kind Lord!
f
mf
dim.
Gra - cious Lord! I pray ____ Thou wilt look on all I love
dim.
p
Ten - der - ly to - day.
p
piacevole

Bring un - to the sor - row - ing
All re - lease from pain, Let the lips of laugh - ter
O - ver - flow a - gain, And with all the need - y

O di - vide, I pray, This vast trea - sure of con - tent
That is mine to - day! Dear Lord, kind Lord!
Gra - cious Lord! I pray Thou wilt look on all I love
Ten - der - ly to - day.
mf
mf
dim.
p
p
mf

The 23rd Psalm

ALBERT HAY MALOTTE

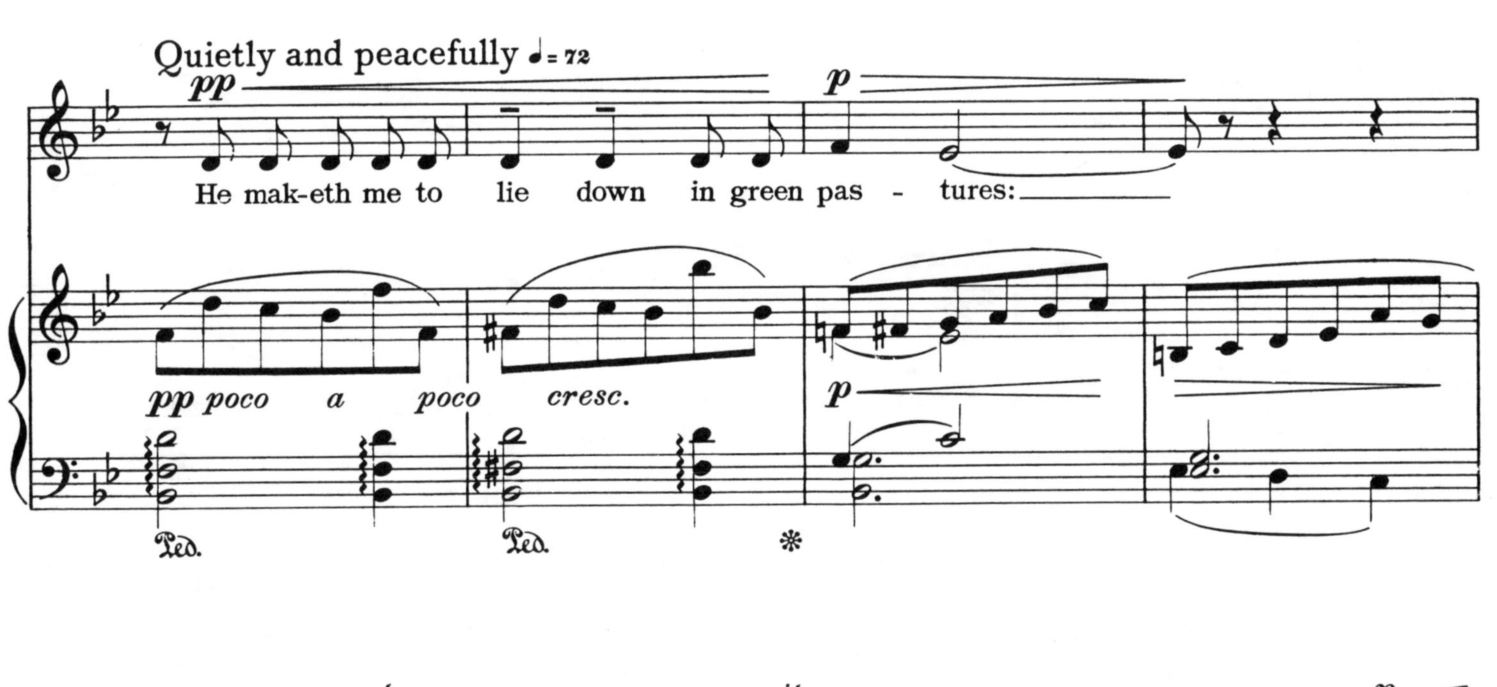
Quietly and peacefully ♩= 72
pp
p
He mak-eth me to lie down in green pas - tures:
pp poco a poco cresc.
p
Ped. Ped.

p ten. pp rit. p
he lead-eth me be-side the still wa - ters. He re-
p ten. pp rit. p
Ped.

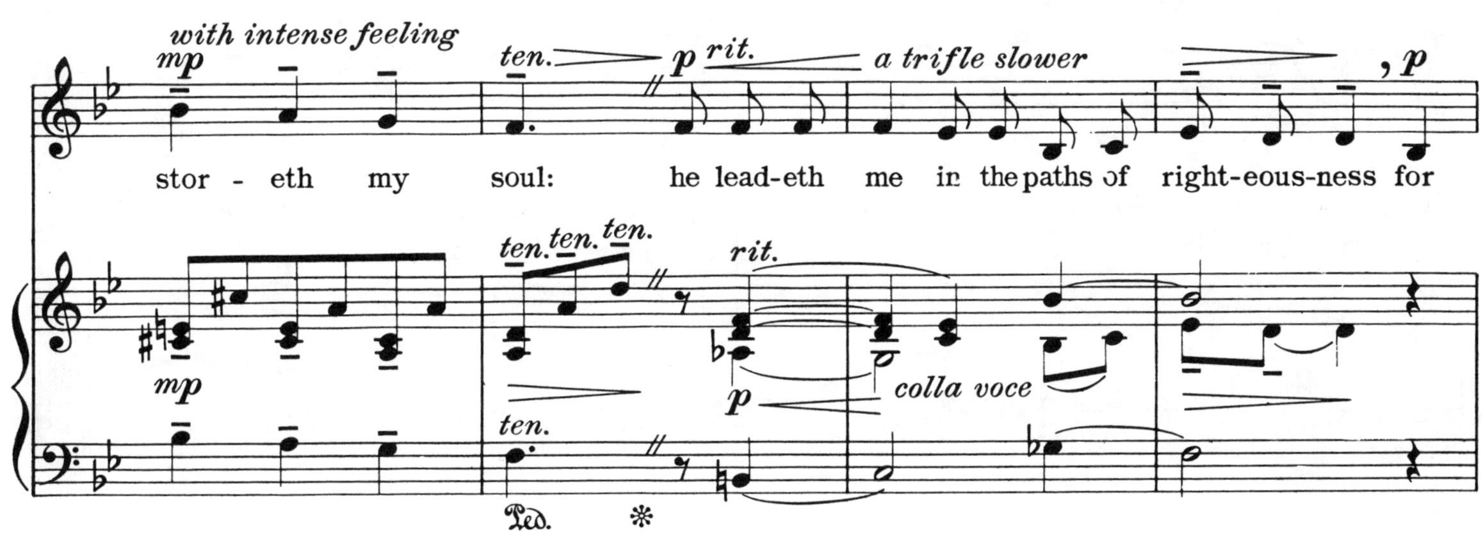
with intense feeling
mp ten. p rit. a trifle slower p
stor - eth my soul: he lead-eth me in the paths of right-eous-ness for
ten. ten. ten. rit.
mp colla voce
ten.
Ped.

tenderly
Adagio (mournfully)
mf
his name's sake.
Yea, tho' I walk thro' the
p
sfz
mp
mf heavily
Ped.
mf poco accel.
f
mp accel.
val - ley of the shad - ow of death,
I will
mf poco accel.
f sostenuto
Ped.
Suddenly much faster (with conviction)
mf
rit. e ten. assai.
fear no e - vil: for thou art with me; thy
mf
rit. e ten. assai.

Molto moderato
mf calmly ten.
rallentando
lunga
mp rit. e ten.
rod and thy staff they com - fort me. Thou pre -
non arp.
ten.
rallentando
fp
Lento (recit.) fervently
ten. ten.
par - est a ta - ble be - fore me in the pres - ence of mine en - e - mies:
fp
faster and with increasing fervor
mf
mp
thou a - noint - est my head with oil, my cup run - neth

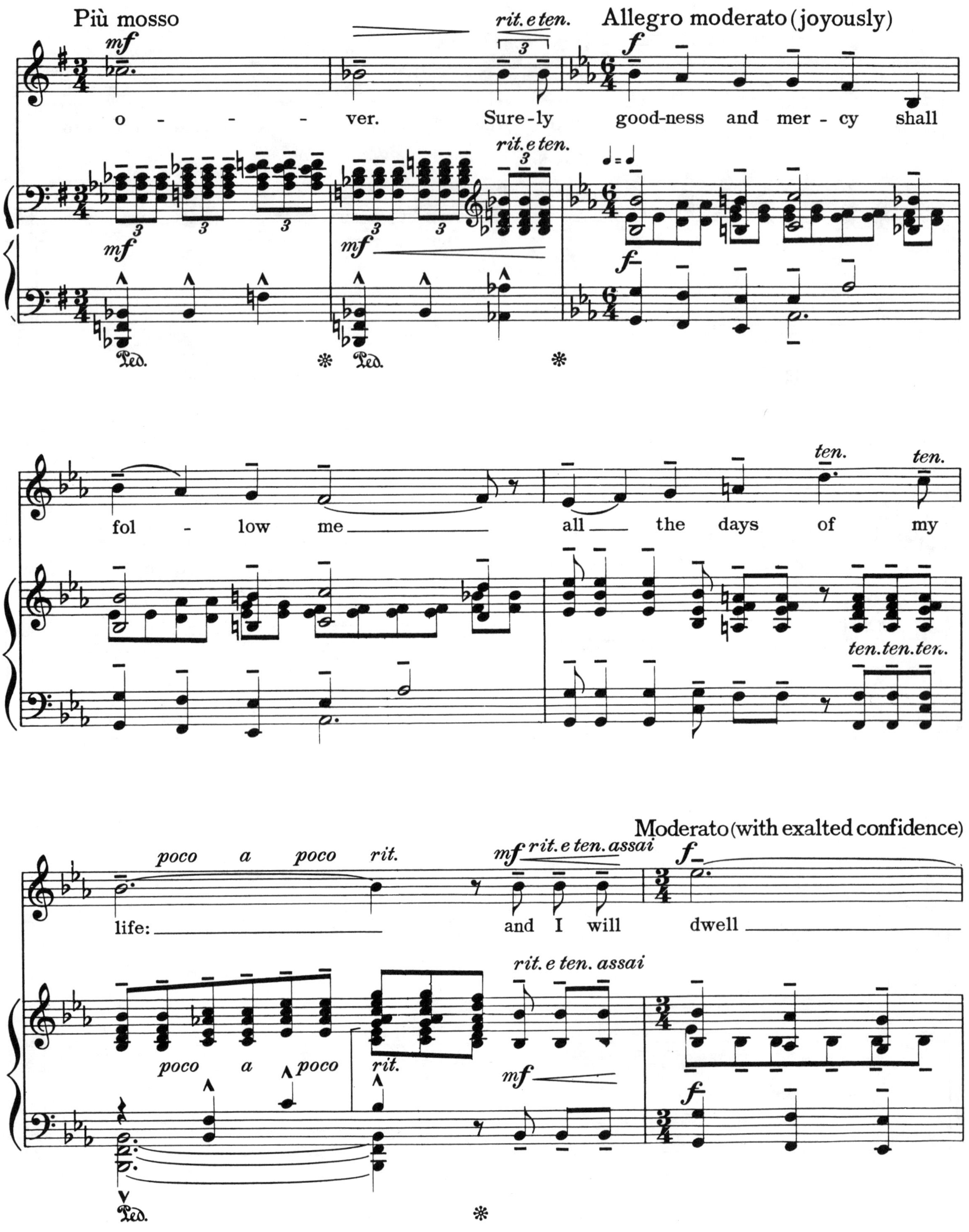

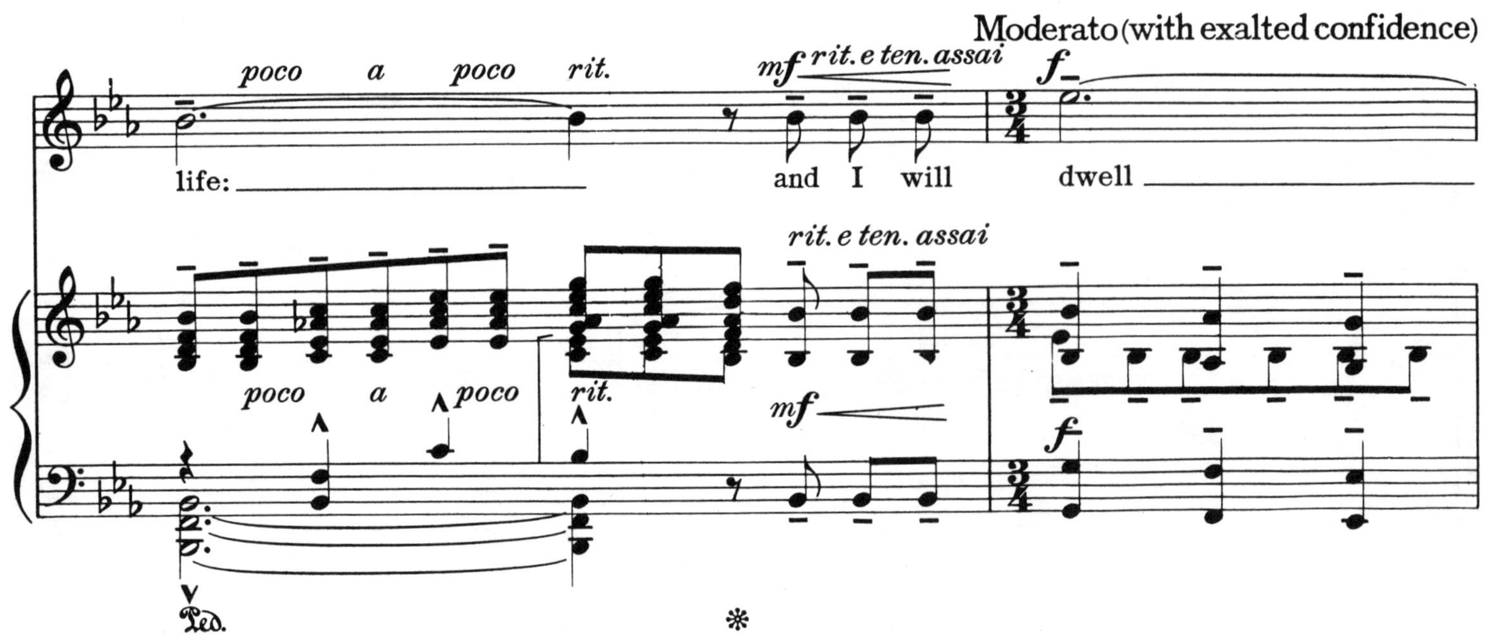

Più mosso
mf
rit. e ten.
Allegro moderato (joyously)
f
o - - - - ver. Sure-ly good-ness and mer - cy shall
rit. e ten.
mf
mf
f
Ped.
Ped.
fol - low me all the days of my
ten.
ten.
ten. ten. ten.
Moderato (with exalted confidence)
poco a poco rit.
mf rit. e ten. assai
f
life: and I will dwell
rit. e ten. assai
poco a poco rit.
mf
f
Ped.

ral - len - tan - do
Very slowly and with great feeling
lunga
in the house of the Lord for
ral - len - tan - do
lunga
Still very slowly
ten.
poco accel.
ev - - - er, and ev - - - er -
l. h.
poco accel.
l. h.
Ped. sostenuto
Ped.
Tempo I° = 72
more.
gradually slower and dying away
ten.
Ped.

Wayfaring Stranger

Words and Music adapted from
The Original Sacred Harp

JOHN JACOB NILES

land to which I go. I'm go-ing there to see my Moth-er, I'm go-ing
there, no more to roam; I'm on-ly go-ing o-ver Jor-dan, I'm on-ly
go-ing o-ver home.
I know dark
clouds will gath-er o'er me, I know my way is rough and steep; Yet beau-teous
mf
mp
mp
mp

fields lie just be - fore me, Where God's re - deemed their vig - ils keep. I'm go - ing
there to see my Fa - ther, He said He'd meet me when I come. I'm on - ly
go - ing o - ver Jor - dan, I'm on - ly go - ing o - ver home.
I want to wear a crown of

glo - ry When I get home to that good land, I want to shout Sal - va - tion's
sto - ry In con-cert with the blood-washed Band. I'm go - ing there to meet my
Sav - iour, To sing His praise for - ev - er - more, I'm on - ly go - ing o - ver
Jor - dan, I'm on - ly go - ing o - ver home.

Were You There?

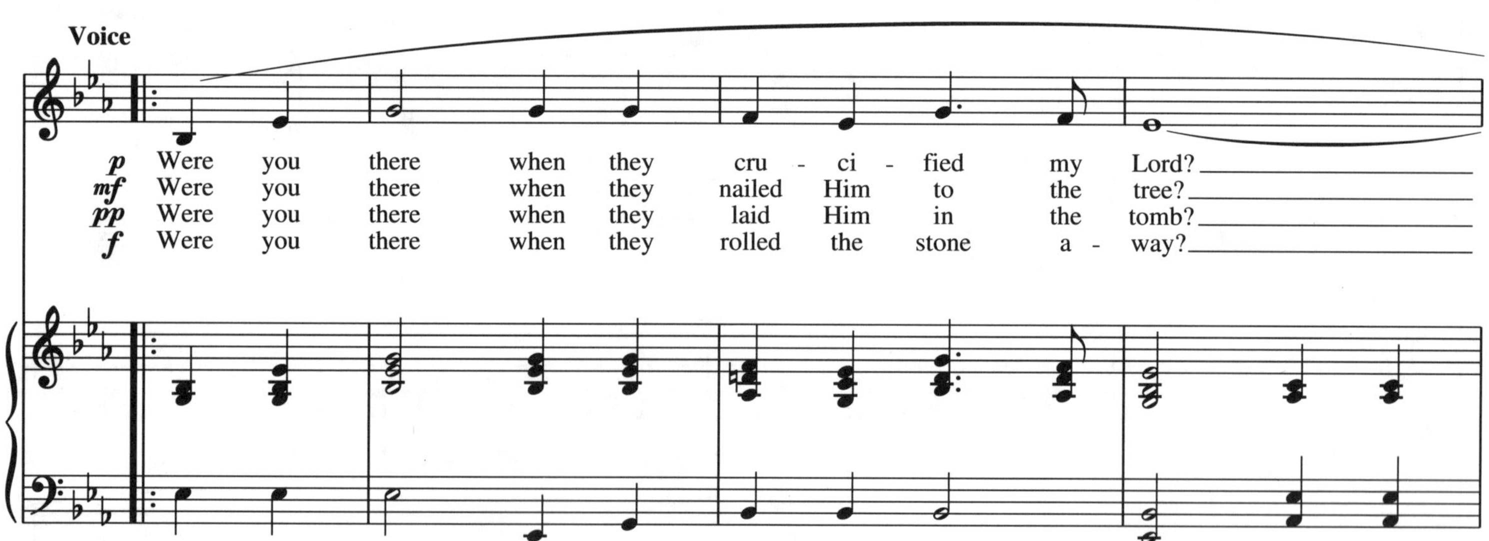

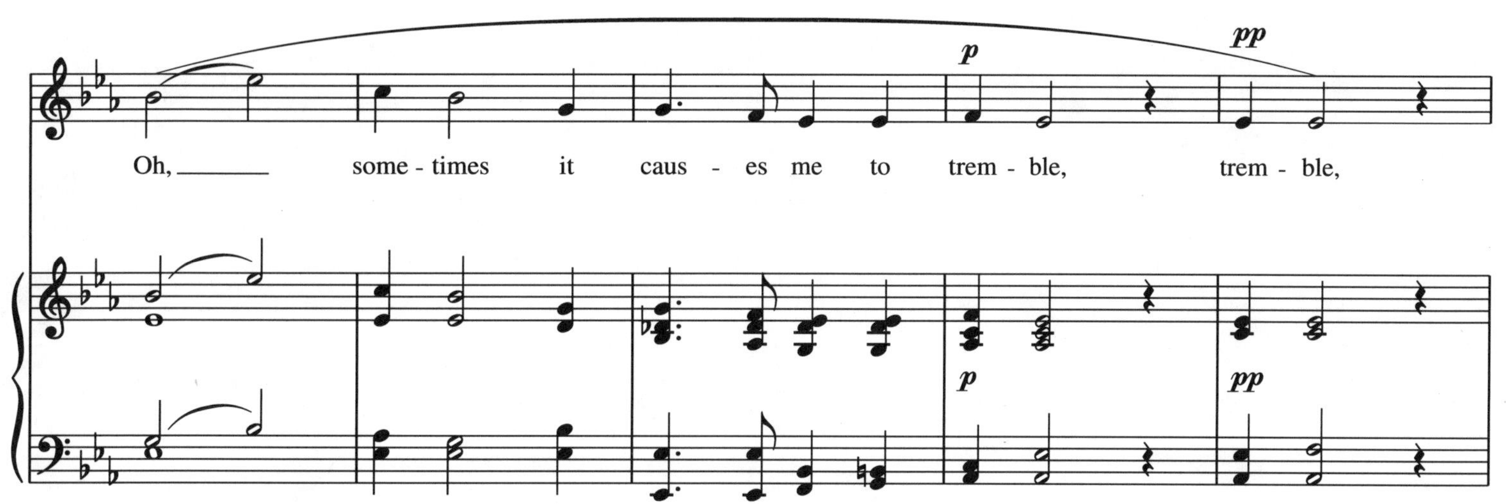

p
pp
Oh, _____ some - times it caus - es me to trem - ble, trem - ble,

trem - ble, _____
Were you there when they cru - ci - fied my
Were you there when they nailed Him to the
Were you there when they laid Him in the
pp Were you there when they cru - ci - fied my

1-3
4
rall.
Lord? _____
tree? _____
tomb? _____
Lord? Were you there?
rall.